Messages from Mooseville

A Year in Alaska

Messages from Mooseville

A Year in Alaska

Leigh Richards

Illustrated by Anne Kinder

Oxford Street Press
Houston, Texas

Jane
Happy birthday!

love & laughter

Kitty Eppston
Leigh Richards
Kathryn Rabinne

Messages from Mooseville
Copyright ©2019 by Leigh Richards

ISBN 978-1-73299858-6-4

Oxford Street Press
Houston, TX

Cover and interior design by Diana Wade

Dedication

In memory of Sarah Brielle,
whose laughter I can still hear in my heart.

And to dearest Richard and Rebecca,
who continue to groan (while smiling) at my puns.

Preface

July 2019

Dear Reader,

Early in 2019, our family purchased a large house that I thought had been emptied by its previous occupants. All the rooms on the first two floors were clean and ready for us to move in, but I thought I would check out the storage area on the top floor. When I climbed the stairs to the hot, dusty third-floor attic, I found three dented cardboard cartons tucked far under the eaves. On the floor alongside the cartons was a piece of notebook paper with *Cleaning Crew—throw away everything in this area* written in pencil. The Scotch tape was dried out; the instructions must have fallen off one of the cartons stacked in the back of the attic. I guess the movers had seen neither the note nor the cartons.

The FedEx labels showed that the cartons were to be delivered to this house address, to a Kitty Eppston. I didn't recognize the name; my husband and I had purchased the house from Lorraine and Alexander

Beaven. The cartons must have been gathering dust in the back of the attic for a very long time. Curious, I opened them. One was full of empty yellowed Tupperware containers. The second contained inexpensive-looking pots and pans in addition to stainless steel flatware. Opening the third carton, I found jumbled piles of woolen scarves and hats, gloves, fishing equipment, ziplock bags filled with feathers, fish bones, and miscellaneous pebbles. At the bottom of the carton was a large stack of papers tied together with a faded pink ribbon. Wanting to read them but not wanting to spend any additional time in the hot attic, I gathered up the packet, locked up the house, and drove to a nearby Starbucks. Latte in hand, I untied the ribbon on the packet and began to read. . . .

As I spewed my mouthful of coffee all over the table laughing out loud, I knew these letters didn't belong in a box at the back of an attic. Both funny and deep, they revealed the thoughts and coping strategies of a woman who was sent, almost twenty-five years before, to live in a world unlike any she had ever experienced.

For weeks I couldn't stop thinking about the letters. What happened to the writer? Was she still living in Houston or had she returned to Alaska? Google showed a Kitty Eppston listed as having attended a variety of Houston fund raisers in years past, but there was no mention of her for almost ten years. Nothing in the obituary records; nothing anywhere at all.

Then my own life and its activities occupied me, and many months went by. In July, our family went to Aspen for a two-week holiday of hiking, biking, and attending the Aspen Music School concerts. I was seated at the Sunday concert next to a slightly chubby, slightly wrinkled, talkative woman. Turned out that before moving to Colorado she had lived in Houston. It couldn't be—but yes, it was Kitty Eppston! I was stunned: what were the odds? I told her I lived in her former Houston house, and that, in the back of the attic, I had found some old cartons addressed to her. Her eyes opened wide, and she put her hand over her mouth. The concert was about to begin, so we made a plan to meet the following morning.

Over coffee at Explore Bookstore and Café, Kitty asked me lots of questions about her former home and garden. She was curious about my life and my career as a psychology professor at the University of Houston. When I tried to steer the conversation to the letters she had written or asked her questions about her year in Alaska, she tried to change the topic. Finally, I admitted to having read her messages from Mooseville. I begged her forgiveness and emphasized my admiration for her coping strategies and determination to see change in a positive way. I asked if I might share her letters with my students and friends.

Kitty finished her coffee and was quiet, seemingly lost in thought. "Well, if you really think my jottings would be helpful to others," she said, "the letters are yours to do with as you choose."

I choose to share them with you.

Leigh Richards

Messages from Mooseville

July 1995

It is past 10:00 p.m. and shafts of Alaskan sunlight are illuminating my desk through the large windows across from me. I am writing a note to go on top of this pile of Xeroxed letters that I'm packing into one of a zillion cartons being shipped back to my Texas home. Years from now when I get around to opening this carton and rereading my letters, I'm sure I'll get a giggle or two remembering all the adventures I had, most unexpectedly and somewhat reluctantly, this year.

I laugh as I write this because I realize the letters that were sent to my friends in the lower forty-eight were really a way of my keeping a diary (I have always sworn, after all, that I would never, ever keep a diary). These letters were my attempt to hold fast to memories of this amazing year.

Just in case years down the road I may have forgotten something about how it all began, I'll add this explanation of who I was and what was happening a little over a year ago.

I was happy as a clam living in Houston, planning our younger daughter's wedding, chairing three fund raisers for "good causes" (as if anyone would fund-raise for a bad cause), attempting to diet so that I would fit into the mother-of-the-bride dress, traveling to the Northeast to visit elderly parents, worrying about our older daughter, who was living in Paris—all the usual midlife Suburban Matron stuff.

My husband, Alan, had been going to Alaska on business several times a month. That commute of his had been going on for a while, and I was getting used to being *"une femme seule"* (as my Paris-based daughter described it). Life was coming along in a predictable way.

Then one day as Alan and I were flying from Houston to San Francisco to host an engagement party for our daughter and her fiancé, the gods laughed. Thirty thousand feet in the air, Alan announced that he was being transferred to Alaska. We were to take up residence there; we were to become Alaskans!

It is neither appropriate nor advisable to scream or faint or murder one's spouse while flying in United States air space. And although I briefly considered all those alternatives, I progressed to my tried and true course of action in times of stress: I started to make lists. Lists of things to be done, of people to contact, of positions to resign, of things to be packed and stored, of things to be packed and shipped . . .

The wedding of my daughter was going to take

place in four months. In the weeks leading up to the wedding, I would organize the house for renters, ship cartons to Alaska, and forget about dieting (after all, I had to have one thing to forget).

The weeks passed in a blur of activities. The fund raisers met their goals. I was able to fit into the mother-of-the-bride dress. My older daughter returned from Paris looking très chic. Museum boards seemed to operate successfully without my attending their meetings. We located a couple who would live in our house for a year or two until we returned to Texas. I compiled more to-do lists.

One of my list items was to empty the pantry, fridge, and freezer. My plan was to eat anything that looked edible and toss the rest. Late one fateful night, I was in the kitchen organizing, discarding, eating . . . when out of the corner of my eye I saw a piece of dark chocolate on the counter. I reached for it to pop into my mouth. The chocolate moved; it moved quickly. I screamed; I screamed loudly. The "chocolate" was a palmetto bug, as we euphemistically call them here in the South—a giant cockroach.

It was time for me to move.

To move to Alaska. And so I did.

9

July 1994

Dear Friends,

I've been in Anchorage almost a month, and that simply does not seem possible. We moved into a three-story contemporary house Alan rented sight unseen. The rental company must not have shown him any photos of the interior of the house. That could be the only explanation for Alan's not preparing me for this massive monstrosity with its built-in velour furniture—all the pieces upholstered in shades of puke green and mustard yellow. There are large-screen TVs everywhere, even over the master bathroom sink and another one in the toilet cubicle. Is one expected just to sit on the commode and watch *Masterpiece Theatre* or *As the World Turns?* Or was the owner of the house just "flush" when he outfitted his home?

This past weekend, Alan and I went on a long car trip. The weather has been gloomy and we hoped to have a few days of adventures in the sunshine. In the summer, Fairbanks is 10–20 degrees warmer than Anchorage, and it's sunny as opposed to the cool drizzle that passes for summer down here. So we journeyed up to Fairbanks for the sun and to be a part of their biggest weekend of the year: Golddust Days. A wide variety of events was scheduled, including the annual World Eskimo and Indian Olympics (WEIO). We spent several hours in the Big Dipper Arena watching some of the Olympic events: the two-foot high kick, in which the winner, using both feet at the same time, kicked a sealskin ball suspended 94 inches in the air! (Note: there was no seal attached to the ball.) The earlobe pull and the crossed-leg skip/jump/hop/lunge are too complicated to even begin to describe.

We were in attendance for the crowning of Miss WEIO, who was selected from a bevy of beauties wearing buckskin, deerskin, heavy fur parkas, and crushed velvet (depending on the tribe represented).

The young woman selected was the conventional type rather than my favorite: the beauty representing Barrow, who sported seal mukluks and a wolverine parka and weighed in at at least 300 pounds. Other activities in Fairbanks included visiting a musk-ox farm at the University of Alaska. We listened to a very long lecture on the musk ox, and now know far more than we will ever need to know. Basic advice: stay out of their way, as they are very territorial. During the September rutting season, the males attack by banging into each other's foreheads with the impact of a car hitting a concrete wall at seventeen mph. Musk-ox foreheads are composed of bone and horn, and the sound of the collision can be heard five miles away. The winning male out-head-butts all the other males in the group, granting him the privilege of being the only one to mate with the females. The other very horny males slink away into the tundra.

The university lecturer also educated us on caribou and reindeer. Did you know that they can (and do) mate with each other, and that their offspring are also fertile and can intermate as well? If the male is a caribou, then the baby is designated a carideer; if the male is a reindeer, then the baby is designated a reinbou. Second-generation possibilities include reinboubou and carideerdeer. I am not kidding. I heard myself softly singing that old nursery rhyme: "Rein, rein go away; caribou another day."

Following the lecture, with our heads packed full of useless information, Alan and I decided to pursue a less cerebral activity and really "play tourist." So we went to Gold Dredge #8, where we panned for gold. The  restored-for-tourists operation features several long waist-high troughs filled with debris on the bottom and muddy, swiftly flowing water. Using large, shallow, circular metal pans, we scooped up some of the pebbles and other debris found in the very cold water. Then, using a circular motion, we were to slosh the debris around in the pans in a way that would allow the water to flow over the sides of the bowl, taking with it the lighter debris, thus leaving in the basin of the bowl the heavier pebbles, aka— hopefully—the gold nuggets. We sloshed; we covered the front of our shirts with muddy water; we looked into the bottom of our pans. Nothing remained. Actually, that is not accurate—what remained for me was a permanently stained blouse and dishpan hands that took several days of anointing with hand lotion to heal. I wonder if gold nuggets might have been found if we had gone to a different location—perhaps Gold Dredge #2 or Gold Dredge #7 . . .

So without any precious metals in our pockets, we continued to explore the summertime offerings of Fairbanks. We went to a farmers' market and saw sixty- to eighty-pound cabbages, gigantic zucchini, and other oversized gourds.

When we asked one of the people selling cabbages why the vegetables were so large, we were told that it was due to the fact that at that time of the year the sun shines almost twenty-four hours a day and the vegetables keep growing day and (lack of) night. Hearing that comment, I had an aha moment. If being in a hot, sunny climate causes normal-size plants to become gigantic-size ones—no extra plant food being required for the huge size and

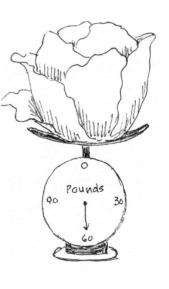

weight gain—then perhaps I finally had an explanation for the weight I'd gained while living in the
sunny South . . .

The following day we visited the Alaska Pipeline
Viewing Station, where my husband, who is, as we say
in Texas, "in the awl bidness," took so many photos he
used up all the film in the camera. I pity our friends
who in the future will have to view our "Year in Alaska"
slide show. While Alan was taking photos, I was getting
eaten alive by giant mosquitoes (their size probably
also attributable to the nonstop sunshine).

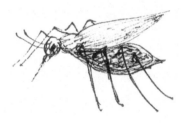

Scratching, I decided that I had seen enough of
the delights of Fairbanks and it was time to return to
Anchorage.

I promise to write you lots of letters this year and
to share with you some of the best of the adventures
this Texas gal (really this Jersey girl) will have had in
Alaska. Right now, I am focused on learning my way

around the city, and how to identify all the various animal tracks I have seen around my house. Very close to my house. Large tracks. Circling the driveway . . . I don't think any of them are carideerdeer tracks or reinboubou tracks, but they could be bear tracks or moose tracks or the tracks of some other large and dangerous beast. I don't have a clue; I need to get a book with photos that identify the animals and their foot/paw/hoof prints so I can determine who might be lurking in the shrubbery.

I will end this long letter. Now I need to locate the post office. The phone book lists the address as 2200 Strawberry; the map shows that street was positioned between Raspberry and Cranberry. (I am berry serious.)

My friends, I miss y'all. I miss our conversations, our long walks together, our jokes, and the groaning when we shared puns. I shall conclude this note with a pun that you may not have heard: As the two earthworms who were looking for moist grass said to each other upon seeing a likely damp spot, "Dew Right."

Hugs,

Me

WELCOME TO
MOOSEVILLE

POP. 250,002

Dear Friends,

Over the past ten days we have had our first visitors: our older daughter, back from Paris and now living in the Big Apple competing for the world record for Most Studious Graduate Student, and our recently married daughter and her husband who live in Texas. All three of them arrived exhausted from their long flights and left exhausted from the tourist marathon we undertook. Was it worth it? Of course!

My neighborhood moose learned through the wild animal vine that I was having house guests, so the first morning, Ms. Moose, approximately nine feet tall, and her two calves (moosettes?) came up to my front walk and proceeded to devour my begonias. When I objected by banging on the front window, Ms. Moose looked up, pawed the ground, and began to amble over to the window, all the while making eye contact with me. With only a pane of glass between us and her red beady eyes staring into my hazel ones, I backed off. Ms. Moose had won Round One of what came to be a definite contest of wills between us. Her two calves were watching their mom's every move and were practicing pawing the ground. I watched divots of grass flying around the front lawn, and then as the three animals sauntered back toward the flower bed together, I became certain of a few things: first, I would always think of them as the Three Mooseketeers; second, in my mind Anchorage would be renamed Mooseville; and third, I would need to do a lot of reading about the habits and dangers of living among moose.

Round Two took place just several days later. With my trunk full of groceries, I slowly drove up my driveway toward the garage. Blocking my entrance were the Three Mooseketeers; they were munching on the begonias and pansies that bordered the driveway. Momma raised her head and glowered at me. Inching the car forward, I glowered back because I had ice cream in the trunk, and it needed to be put into the freezer. Momma took a step or two toward my car. I tapped the horn, and two of the Three Mooseketeers ran away from the driveway. Momma took a running step toward my car, thrust out her hoof, and bashed the side of the hood. Only then did she join her two calves on the lawn. I drove into the garage, shut the door, and sat in the car to catch my breath. Getting out of the car, I saw the dent. Clearly in this, Round Two, I was de-feeted.

Not as intimidating as the moose but just as impressive were all the salmon we saw in the midst of spawning. Although watching salmon spawn is a popular Alaskan pastime, I feel that there is a Masters-and-Johnson voyeuristic quality to the viewing. How would we feel if fish watched us? But the Mooseville residents seem to have a prurient interest in fish sex, and a significant number of people wear T-shirts that read: S*pawn till you die.* A true statement for the salmon, but not a shirt I wanted my new son-in-law to purchase, even though he did seem very interested in watching the salmon . . .

As many of you know (although you may deny it) a very popular how-to book from a few years back was titled *The Joy of Sex*, a play on the popular cookbook *The Joy of*

Cooking. Because I've been doing a lot of salmon cooking and the fish are in the midst of nonstop spawning, I think there must be a *Joy of* book that can combine the two events. I wonder what the title might be . . .

When we tired of watching the salmon, we were able to focus on other animals seen in the waters around Mooseville. There are sea otters, whales, and a variety of salmon—pink, red, silver, and king—as well as trout and other fish, including that country-and-western-singing fish—the Dolly Varden. Was it a Dolly Varden that I heard singing to the spawning salmon: "Roe, roe, roe and float, gently down the stream"?

Although the weather has been glorious, it gets VERY cold when one is near the water. When we went to spend a day on a whale-watching boat, I warned everyone to wear long underwear, sweaters, parkas, gloves, etc. Did they believe me? What do you think? I dressed as if I were going to Siberia in February. The rest of the family, attired in clothes they would wear during summer in the lower forty-eight, didn't do much walking around the boat because they had to huddle up together to stay warm. I didn't move much either, because I was wearing so many layers, I couldn't even bend my knees. But we had a good time on the whale-watching boat nonetheless; in truth, we had a whale of a good time.

On another excursion we saw several glaciers and took a several-hour ferry ride across Prince William Sound. In Whittier, we had a three-hour wait between the car-train and the ferry. What to do in Whittier? There is one high-rise building there. Inside the building there are apartments, a post office, a restaurant, a barbershop, a bowling alley, and a museum. It reminded me of some dorms at the University of Texas; one never needs to leave the building. The rest of the town consists of two espresso bars, one café, a fuel-tank farm, and an all-purpose general store with a Pavlovian trained reindeer named Beau in a fenced yard. If one puts a quarter into the reindeer food machine, Beau comes leaping out of his shelter, pink nostrils all adrool, looking for a handout.

Enough about Whittier; suffice it to say that there is a song I heard at the Fly By Night Club here in Mooseville that begins, "Nothing could be shittier than to find yourself in Whittier in the morning."

After the newlyweds returned to Texas, the graduate student had a few more days to stay and play. So we decided to have a true Alaskan adventure and go on a fishing trip. I drove several hours down the Kenai Peninsula and stopped at a fishing cabin that provided basic (v-e-r-y basic) evening accommodation together with a guide and boat for the following day's fishing. The alarm went off in our rustic cabin in time for us to reach the four-person boat at 5:30 a.m. There was much complaining. We fished the river in the very cold early hours of the morning. There was more complaining. Then my daughter caught her first salmon—euphoria! In truth, both my daughter and the salmon were hooked! The day's fishing adventure resulted in our catching several pink salmon, and I caught a thirteen-pound silver salmon. We hated to get off the boat, but it was time to return to Mooseville. We were taught how to fillet our catch, and then, with the fish in a cooler, we drove the three hours back to Mooseville, feeling like the mighty hunters and providers of dinner that we were. I enjoyed every morsel until we began to discuss how much each delicious bite actually cost: the overnight in the cabin, the fishing guide and boat charter, driving three hours each way, etc. Ah, but who could put a price on the thrill of the chase and the excitement of the catch? (Actually my husband could . . . and did.)

Okay—I've been sharing my happening—what are all of you doing? I know you are all involved in a zillion different things. Send a letter to your friend living in the Last Frontier. Those are the two words printed on my Alaska license plate. Being from Houston, I had thought that the Last Frontier was outer space; I must have been brainwashed by NASA.

Hugs,

Me

Dear Friends,

Termination Dust has fallen on the mountains surrounding Mooseville—now hasn't that given you a visual image of Arnold Schwarzenegger tromping around the glaciers? Well, rest easy; Termination Dust is the local term for the first snow of the season. I must say that I find snow in September to be a more alarming thought than Big Arnold any day. The geese are gathered in gaggles (don't you love that descriptor?) practicing their V's. You may not know that geese spend their early summer days in Alaska attempting to determine which letters of the alphabet would serve them best as they fly long distances. The B and the S formations are especially funny to watch for their aerodynamic ineptness. (The Alaskans say: "Take a gander at that formation" and then they giggle at the gaggle.)

These past several weeks, the geese have focused their efforts on W and V and are making great efforts to select the correct letter so they can escape any additional Termination Dust and fly down to Texas, to greet all the eager hunters who are patiently waiting in bird blinds.

(A question just entered my mind: In Italy, do hunters shoot birds from Venetian blinds?) Attempting to select the correct letter of the alphabet must cause the birds some stress and even, perhaps, some collisions. There were many feathers to be found on our lawn, and I have saved some of the prettiest ones.

We live in the flatlands section of Mooseville, and as of yet we have not had any snow and are still enjoying the autumn scenery. The leaves on the trees have turned golden, the shrubs are russet, and in the distance we can see the  snow-topped mountains. It is beautiful and relaxing. Relaxing, that is, unless you are in the way of a galloping moose. The moose are galloping because it is rutting season and hunting season. For moose it must be sort of a good-news-bad-news joke. Just last evening, Alan and I saw a flash of a moose running across our lawn. Then we saw an enormous bull moose with a huge rack—antlers for all you lower forty-eighters—in hot pursuit. Around the back lawn he went, crashing through and completely flattening the shrubbery, in search of his reluctant moosette. It gave a new meaning to the phrase *She went to rack and ruin.*

Rack of moose reminds me of food. Of course, everything reminds me of food. . . . Most newspapers have a weekly food/recipe section; no exception is the Mooseville paper. However, the recipes are considerably different from those I have seen anywhere else. In this land of fresh fish and even fresher moose, Spam is a popular food item. Okay, I will concede that Spam and eggs, Spamburgers, and Spam nachos are arguably acceptable—but Spam desserts? In this year's Alaska State Fair cooking contest, the winning recipe for a Spam dessert (!!!) was Spam Holiday Truffles, where spam was combined with coconut, rum, and chocolate. Perhaps if there is enough rum . . . ? Another published prizewinning recipe is titled Spice Cream. Yes, you read the previous sentence correctly: the recipe is for Spam ice cream! The ingredients in Spam are water, potato starch, salt, sugar, and pork. I guess if you add cream, go heavy on the sugar, finely mince the Spam, and freeze the mixture, it actually could become something that could be scooped into a cone and be deemed "delish." But I think I'll stick to vanilla or chocolate-chip ice cream for my cones.

Still on the subject of food, I'm going to educate you about Alaskan vegetables. As I wrote to you last month, vegetables here are large. How large is large? Well, when I asked a friend if he was going to attend the Alaska State Fair in the nearby town of Palmer, his response was "No, the zucchini makes me feel inadequate." As I mentioned in an earlier letter, here in Alaska the cabbages weigh sixty to eighty pounds, turnips are the size of cabbages sold in the lower forty-eight, and the yellow squash and zucchini are truly awesome, weighing in at ten to eighteen pounds! In New York City and Houston, people shop in expensive stores for designer clothes—Bill Blass, Ungaro, Givenchy . . . In Mooseville, people shop in expensive stores for designer vegetables. My local supermarket offers me "lettuce grown by Ben Vanderwheels" and "cucumbers by Vitali Seldovich" at inch-by-inch prices to match those of Givenchy and Chanel.

I'm certain that it is not easy to grow designer lettuce, because Mooseville is seemingly a major site for slugs. I'm not talking about slugs from handguns; I refer to the fat, slimy wormlike creatures that leave trails of silver mucus all over my paths, the slugs that eat triple their weight in flower petals and hosta plants every day. Perhaps there are so many slugs because there are so many leaves of gargantuan vegetables for them to eat. Perhaps there are more dangerous and destructive animals for Alaskans to kill than slugs, and thus the slugs are able to flourish in their slimy, gluttonous bliss. But in my own garden, the begonias that the moose did not eat, the slugs did. They even slimed my geraniums and marigolds. I don't understand how it is possible that the mucus-clad slug thrives in a climate that is too cold for snakes, fleas, ticks, etc. Alaskan slugs might be related to the Alaska ice worm, a small black worm that lives in glacier ice and dines on pollen that settles on the surface of the ice. Currently the Japanese are buying glacier ice and packaging it for very expensive ice cubes. I guess that getting a worm in one's drink would be considered a treat—just an extra bit of raw protein to go with one's sushi order.

Hugs,

Me

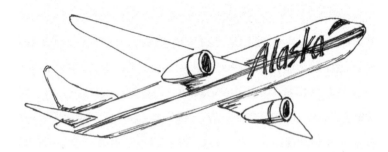

Dear Friends,

I know you have already received a September letter from me, but there is just so much information to share about our adventures here in Alaska that I decided I would write you twice this month. That way you can pace yourselves and not get exhausted from the gales of laughter I am told occur whenever you rip open my envelopes and begin reading.

I'll start this letter telling you about the journeys Alan and I have taken during this past month. We signed up for a small group tour and flew three hours north on Alaska Airlines (factoid: no other state has an airline company named after it) to get to Kotzebue, a city above the Arctic Circle. City is probably too grandiose a word for Kotzebue, because it doesn't have any paved streets, and all the homes, stores, schools, etc. are built on top of the permafrost. The group tour began with a long walk across the cold and windy tundra, learning which berries were poisonous and which were not. Then we were given time to gather berries and eat them. No one seemed to be hungry. . . .

Later in the day, we attended a cultural presentation organized by a dozen citizens of Kotzebue who were dressed in traditional garb—brightly colored clothing trimmed with fur and quills. I greatly enjoyed watching the games and dancing until I, and I alone, was brought down from the bleacher seating to perform with the native dancers. I was suspicious that my husband had paid extra money to ensure that I would be selected for this honor. I can't send you a video, because he was laughing so hard he couldn't focus the camera to put the "Kitty Eppston sees a walrus and alerts her tribe to come for harpooning" interpretive dance on film. The people in our tour group gave me a standing ovation (unless of course they were just ready to leave the bleachers for the next adventure). I never saw a newspaper review of my performance, but I am convinced that the shaking of my own personal muktuk added an extra je ne sais quoi to the performance that was greatly appreciated by the natives.

That evening after the performance, we flew south to Nome, where people were panning the sand for gold and camping in tents staked out on the beach, despite the fact that it was very cold, with a wind chill factor far below freezing. I had heard of "gold fever" but I had never heard the term "gold frostbite" before we visited Nome. Alan and I also went to a "tourist" gold mine and did some digging. Now my husband has four flakes of 24-karat gold, each the size of a bit of dandruff, to prove his mining prowess. In this, my second mining attempt, I didn't get dandruff, but I did again get chapped and very dirty hands. I also picked up a few pretty pebbles, clearly not gold nuggets, to put in my pocket to take home as a souvenir.

Not one single tree grows in the entire city of Nome, and there is only one paved street. We were told that a very popular recreational activity of the (Nome-ites? Nomians? Nomenclatures?) locals is to drive for forty-five minutes to look at the only tree that can be found for many, many miles.

I have been thinking about Fred Rogers, who wrote a song for the children addicted to his program *Mr. Rogers' Neighborhood.* An excerpt of the libretto is: "Tree tree tree; tree tree, tree, tree tree tree, tree tree tree, we love you, yes we do, tree tree tree . . ." Perhaps instead of being a native

Pennsylvanian, Fred Rogers is really a Nomian.

On another September weekend, Alan and I flew for two hours south of Mooseville to Baranof Island and the fishing town of Sitka. We had been told that the area was very beautiful and lush, but it was foggy and rainy and we couldn't really see anything except gray skies, gray vistas, and gray water. We had an interesting time doing all the inside things—museums and churches. It was in one of the museums that we learned all about the Tlingit Indians, who were the original inhabitants of the area before the Russians arrived. The Tlingit make up a significant percent of the population in the southeastern part of Alaska, and recently made the national press when a judge allowed the local tribe to sentence two teenagers who had committed a violent crime to a year in isolation on a deserted island, instead of being sent to prison. We learned that the *T* in the word *Tlingit* is pronounced as if it were a *K*. My husband pointed out that I could spell my first name *Titty* and be linguistically correct in that area of Alaska. As much as I enjoy being a part of the local scene, I don't think it is a spelling I will use as part of my signature.

After one and a half days in Sitka, we were ready to return to the delights of the big city of Mooseville, but we almost weren't able to do that. It was not possible for our plane to land because of heavy fog. It was a tense time (past, present, and future) when we learned that we might be staying in Sitka indefinitely, or at least until the arrival of the next flight scheduled for the following day. Happily for us, and for the others waiting forlornly and rather wetly on the tarmac, the sun made an appearance for a few minutes, and the pilot made a dramatic landing into Sitka. Passengers disembarked the small plane, and those of us on the tarmac ran onto the plane, and took off, heading back to Mooseville.

For the following weekend's trip, we decided not to rely on small planes for our mode of transport; instead we drove with some friends to our next adventure spot. We drove and drove and drove down to the end of the Kenai Peninsula until we reached the Homer Spit. Sounds like an episode of *The Simpsons*. But because the narrow piece of land on Kachemak Bay was surrounded by extraordinarily beautiful scenery, we discarded our mental image of the Simpsons clearing their throats and expectorating, and instead we focused on the beauty of Mother Nature. Under sunny blue skies, we saw aqua-hued water surrounded by snowcapped mountains. We toured the Coastal

Environmental Center and saw cockles leap into the air and really move when approached by starfish. This was not a ho-hum event; those cockles really move quickly and for long distances. Who knew? Maybe that old Irish song's original lyrics were "Cockles have muscles, alive, alive oh."

We didn't move as quickly as a cockle when we hiked in what was billed as a virgin forest. We walked slowly, looking down at the path, just in case there were roots or rocks that would cause us to fall. One of our visiting friends, an ob-gyn, questioned the term "virgin" forest after we saw several used and discarded condoms in the parking area adjacent to the path. Avoiding the detritus, we hiked on the trail through the woods and found ourselves carefully walking around piles of bear scat. Scat in this situation doesn't mean go away; rather it is an official term for another four-letter word that starts with *s*. No matter what one calls the brown piles, I was not thrilled to see them. I never wanted to encounter a large bear up close and personal—neither the "friendly" black bear nor the "killer" brown bear. However, former Girl Scout that I was, I had prepared for the hike and brought with me my husband's Alyeska Pipeline Company anti-bear whistle (a gift from the company to their employees).

You better believe I tweeted that whistle for the duration of the hike. We all had headaches by the time we were done, but we had no bear trouble.

Several days later at the Mooseville Zoo, I tested the whistle in front of the cages of both the black and the brown bears.

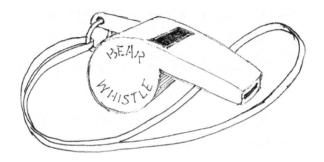

There was not one iota of reaction from any of the animals. One of the bears even came closer to me in an attempt to determine what was making that lovely sound. So much for free gifts from Alyeska Pipeline Company. We could have been mauled in the woods if there had been aggressive ursines nearby. My whistle tweets would not have prevented carnage. Interestingly, I recently have read about the company having a lot of problems with lawsuits filed by whistle-blowers. (See the business sections of your local newspaper.)

I have so much more to tell you, but I must sign off; it is late and I can bearly stay awake.

Hugs from your friend,

Kitty (note I haven't used the Tlingit spelling)

Dear Friends,

Another new experience to add to my list: fishing in the rain. To be more specific, fishing in the cold rain in a drift boat wearing four layers of clothing, topped off with hip boots and a life vest. If you can imagine the Pillsbury Doughboy wearing a sou'wester trying to lift one leg high enough to get into a flat-bottomed boat without toppling over into a racing river, you are beginning to visualize the scene that took place in the early dawn hours on a recent Saturday. Once in the two-person boat, I realized why it is called a flat-bottomed boat: that is the formation the passenger's derriere takes on after ten minutes of sitting on the metal seat. The boat is also known as a drift boat—a surprise indeed, since that name would indicate that the passenger might enjoy a leisurely and gentle bob down the river. Not the case. First, the fishing guide rowed like crazy against the Kenai River's current, and then we raced through white water, holding on to our fishing poles. I clutched my fishing pole between my two well-padded legs and held tightly to the sides of the boat while whispering a few intensely focused prayers. While one of us in the boat was praying, the other was saying that the next set of rapids was *really* the faster water. Not your normal fishing trip—if you catch my drift.

You might be wondering about the whereabouts of my husband. The answer is that Alan was asleep in bed at the lodge. When the alarm clock rang in the pitch darkness of the room and we could hear the rain pouring down on the roof he announced: "Time to get dressed, fisherperson." Then he laughed, turned over, and went back to sleep.

What did I catch, while Alan lay snug in bed, not worrying about being swept away by white water? Many rainbow trout, all under the legal limit and thus not allowed to be kept, and a miserable head cold that I *did* keep.

The fishing adventure took place earlier this month when I thought it was cold. Now, in late October, I know what chilly autumn weather in Alaska really is—below freezing both day and night. Of course the issue of what is day and what is night is getting very subjective. It is still totally dark at 9:15 a.m., and residents of Mooseville are losing an amazing amount of daylight per week. Now snow and ice are on the ground. Additionally there is something alarming called black ice that is invisible but appears on streets and sidewalks when least expected. The other morning after I "steered into the skid" (remember your driver's education lessons?) several times on the way out of our driveway, I heard the radio DJ say: "Black ice has arrived." I thought he was talking about a rock band, especially when he continued "Remember that black ice requires heavy metal studs. Have you gotten yours?" No, I hadn't. But then Paul Simon was not wearing heavy metal studs when he sang "Slip Slidin' Away."

In my last letter to you, I forgot to mention that when Alan and I were in Sitka we visited a raptor rehabilitation center. Didn't Gilbert and Sullivan write "Oh joy, oh raptor unforeseen"? What was unforeseen for us was that our national symbol really is a smelly bird. Put several bald eagles in one room, and oh, what a stink! The eagles' usual diet is rodent-on-the-run. The birds ingest the fur and the bones, digest some of it, and the remainder of the bits and pieces that are not digested are spewn far and wide. Wear a hat and keep your mouth closed when you go visit eagles! In addition to eating rodents, the raptors will also carry off small dogs and cats. As will coyotes.

Why am I raising the issue of coyotes? I write you about coyotes because the October 17, 1994, front-page headline of the *Anchorage Daily News* read: "Coyotes Head for Trouble." It seems that the coyote population here is at an all-time high and, not content with eating small animals of all types, the coyotes (or one very persistent coyote) have attempted to eat several Mooseville residents. So many questions come to mind—how large was the coyote (or the coyotes)? How small were

the people? Where were the people at the time of the attacks? Did they attempt to outrun the coyote? Could I outrun a coyote while wearing my current layered fashion look of thermal long underwear, slacks, turtleneck, sweater, boots, down parka, insulated gloves, and floppy fleece hat? Doubtful.

But my biggest question of all is: what was the exact meaning of the newspaper headline?

I think that I will add another layer to my fashionable ensemble after the middle of next month, when the concealed gun law goes into effect. Anyone who gets a special license will be allowed to carry a concealed handgun. (Why are they called handguns? To the best of my knowledge there are no foot guns.) Worried that I would be the only Mooseville resident without a gun, I decided to take lessons just in case I choose to become a pistol-packing mama. The only accredited course here is one established by the NRA; I swallowed my pacifistic disapproval and went to register for the twelve-hour "Learn How to Protect Yourself and Your Loved Ones" course. I privately dubbed it the "Aim and Maim" class. Imagine my indignation when I was not allowed to take the class. Did the NRA know of my former membership in the ACLU? Had they tracked my giving record to the Sarah Brady Gun Control Bill? Nope. It was as simple as the fact that only those with Alaska driver's licenses have the right to carry a concealed weapon. The rest of us can only wear Kevlar and hope that the person next to us in the supermarket checkout line isn't a psychopath.

Maybe it's the long hours of darkness that are giving me my current obsession with death. But whether I'm munched on by a coyote or riddled with bullets is not as much of a worry as is death by noshing (which in the past would have been one of my favorite ways to depart this world). It was my very own doctor from Houston who was caring enough to send me an article that has been instrumental in changing the way I plan our dinner selections. It seems that an outbreak of shigellosis occurred after several families in an Alaskan village had eaten moose soup. Doctors, never willing to let the odd enteric pathogen go unresearched, have now tracked botulism outbreaks to additional Alaskan gustatory delights such as fermented beaver tail, muktuk (whale blubber with attached skin), and seal flipper. [To prove that I am not making this stuff up please review the following citations: West J Med 1990; 153:390-393 and 1994; 160:430-433.] Seal flipper? Is it stewed, baked, or sautéed? Neither my Julia Child nor Craig Claiborne cookbooks had a recipe for seal flipper. I guess the recipe must be available on a need-to-know basis. Fortunately, one Mooseville delicacy, halibut cheeks on hamburger buns, is not on the botulism alert list. Just FYI, whenever I eat my dinner of cheeks and buns, I get an urge to join a gym to exercise my gluteus maximus.

Although I don't belong to a gym and I was unable to enroll in "Aim and Maim," I did successfully register for an all-women fly-fishing course.

The course will be taught by a registered fly-fishing guide with the comforting first name of Pudge. I have confidence that she will teach me well, and that in short order I might be fishing with Robert Redford and Brad Pitt in their sequel movie, *A River Runs Next to It.* In anticipation of learning how not to tangle my line in the shrubbery, I purchased all sorts of fishing equipment. And in order to be the teacher's pet, I bought a dozen of Pudge's hand-tied flies. They range from a purple pipe-cleaner type thing with little elastic bands sticking out in all directions to objects that look like the dust bunnies I find under my sofas and beds. I can't imagine a self-respecting fish wanting to munch on a dust bunny, but Pudge insisted that they are the most spectacular flies. If I can't trust someone named Pudge, then who am I going to trust—Twiggy?

Sticking (sorry I know I had promised several of you that I wood knot end with a bad pun) to my resolve to keep this October letter to as few pages as possible, I'll resist going on any more tangents and will sine off . . .

Hugs,

Me

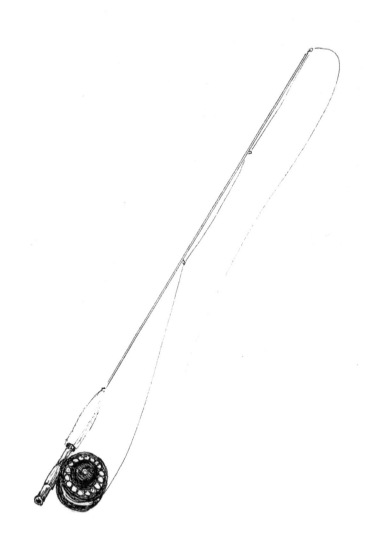

November 1994

Dear Friends,

Did Juneau that the Alaska state capital is accessible only by air or ship? Did Juneau that the city has less than twenty-seven thousand residents? (Mooseville has ten times as many people.) Now you do. Alan and I flew to Juneau this past weekend so that we could play tourist again. After four hours, we had driven or walked down every road, visited the churches, museums, and taken the requisite photo of the Mendenhall Glacier, and we still had thirty-six hours left before we were scheduled to leave on our flight back to Mooseville. The legislature was not in session, the governor was out of town, and there was not a single lobbyist in the hotel lobby. We spent a lot of time in the Red Dog Saloon.

One of the odd things we noticed in Juneau was an interesting sign in our hotel room: *If you need to dispose of syringes, please contact the front desk.* I have heard the phrase "bloodsucking politicians" but thought it was hyperbole, not a medical statement. Are the users of the syringes politicians with diabetes? In constant pain? Shooting up serious drugs? I wonder if the signs are a standard feature in hotels all over the USA where lobbyists and politicians stay? Or is this an Alaska thing? When next you are in a hotel in Austin or DC or some other political paradise, do check out the signage.

I am now in the third week of my fly-fishing course with Pudge. Each class, held in a large community-center gymnasium, is three hours long, and my head is reeling (no pun intended) but with facts, positions, and cautions—somewhat analogous to what I experienced in my junior-high sex-education class. There is so much equipment one needs to acquire, and most of it is slightly different for Alaskan waters than for other fishing locations. I will summarize.

If I wanted to invest in equipment, I would need: two four-piece graphite rods and their metal cases. One rod would weigh five pounds and be used to fish for trout and grayling; the other rod would weigh nine pounds and be used for silver salmon. The rods could either have fast or medium action, depending upon my preference (getting back to that sex ed class again). Just as fly fishers have a different rod for trout and salmon, they also have a reel matched to each rod. To quote from my instructor: "Reels should have an exposed rim to permit you to palm the reel to increase drag when necessary." Exposed rim? Increase drag? I have the feeling that I am entering the netherworld of S&M bars, not sandbars. But I digress. I must have two spools for each reel, and the spools will have both their backing and their fly lines put on at the store after I have decided whether I want a floating line, a sinking-tip line, or a floating line with split shot. Then I need to purchase several types of monofilament line so that I can knot my own butt and tippet (giggle, giggle). I was told that someone at the store would be willing to knot my butt for an extra fee . . . but I chose not to have that done.

Knots—what a difficult thing for a person with trifocals to master. The monofilament is almost invisible, and there are a zillion steps for each of the three different knots one must use. Although I won't attempt to describe the procedures, I will allow the names of the knots to speak for themselves. First is the nail knot (by the time I finish tying this one, I have few fingernails still intact). Then there is the blood knot (no comment), and finally the improved clinch knot. This last one ties the fly to the tippet.

Flies, like people, come in all different weights, colors, and shapes. The trick is to discover what the fish are eating the week that you'll be fishing and then create a construction of feathers, elk hair, chenille, and foil to resemble something that looks like the fish food du jour. Some professionally constructed flies imitate various stages in the life cycle of certain insects, so one needs to have faux larvae, nymphs, and flies, as well as faux eggs and faux rotting fish flesh. One of the most popular dry flies used in this area of Alaska is named the egg-sucking leech. I do hope that I never encounter a real one of those creatures.

Now just in case these artistic creations get wet (of course they will get wet, the fisherperson is casting them into the river!), one must also have a jar of Gink (actual trademarked name) to rub on the fly when it stops floating. Attached to the bottom of the fly is a hook. Hooks differ by length, strength, and by the size of the gap between the barb and the bend of the hook. The larger the number of the hook, the smaller the actual fly. (For all of us females in the class, that last sentence seemed like such a typical male thing.) Doesn't all the equipment required to fly-fish make putting a worm on a hook that dangles off a piece of string seem the easier and better way to fish? Except, of course, to the worm.

I have not shared with you all the various clothing specific to fly-fishing that is deemed necessary;

perhaps I will do that another time. I shall end this letter with an amazing happening. One of the local fishing guide services has published a large photo of me taken earlier this fall. Happily wearing incorrect fishing attire, I am holding a large silver salmon on the cover of their fishing brochure. I caught the salmon using a rod of unknown weight with the metal hook of the rod threaded with real salmon eggs. And I didn't have to use any Gink at all.

Being the cover girl on a fishing brochure sent around the world makes me wonder if this constitutes my fifteen minutes of fame. Or is this only the beginning? Check out future issues of *Reel and Lure* and *Fishing Paradise*. Of course, I'd much rather appear in that erudite fishing journal: *Hook, Line, and Thinker*.

Hugs from
the Alaska Sunrise Fishing cover girl,

Me

December 1994

Dear Friends,

It is now December, dark dark dark December. Currently in Mooseville the sun rises at 10:12 a.m. and sets at 3:41 p.m. Santa's reindeer are really going to need to depend on Rudolph's red glowing nose to light the way. We all know that candy canes and gingerbread are traditional holiday sweets, but I decided that I would try to satisfy my holiday sweet tooth by eating ice cream. There are many brands sold in Mooseville that are not found in Houston supermarkets. One new premium (expensive) ice cream has just arrived at the supermarkets here in time for this holiday season. It came packaged in a square box with the label: Alaska Ice Cream. Also printed on the box was a lengthy statement:

Alaska represents the best nature has to offer—clean air, sparkling water and ice untouched for centuries. Alaska also stands for a way of life in harmony with the natural world: unhurried, willing to slow down and do things the right way. And to enjoy them once they're done. As the makers of Alaska Ice Cream, we want you to know why no other ice cream tastes like Alaska.

There was an Anchorage address on the box. I was suspicious because it seemed a bit over the top. I thought there was a strong possibility that the PR writer had been under the influence of something stronger than ice cream when writing about "the taste of Alaska." I did some sleuthing and discovered that the address of the company was a private post office box in a local mall. Sleuthing some more, I learned the ice cream is produced in Long Island City in New York! We all know what NYC stands for as "a way of life." And as for the taste of Long Island City . . . well, the ripe, robust crunchiness of a landfill comes to my mind, but fortunately, thanks to my sleuthing, it will not come to my palate.

Earlier this month, Alan and I journeyed to Vancouver, British Columbia, for a three-day weekend. Vancouver is a wonderful city to visit, with beautiful mountains, sparkling water, moss-covered forests, and spacious parks. (Hey—I could get a job writing copy and PR for an ice cream company!) One of the habitats in the lovely Vancouver Aquarium housed killer whales—orcas. I knew that the whales were large, black on top, and white on the bottom, and that they lived in cold northern waters. What I didn't know was that the gestation time for a baby orca is seventeen months.

At the time of our visit, the female orca at the aquarium was sixteen months pregnant. She swam around in the large pool and seemed in amazingly good spirits until the male started to approach her. The aquarium staff person said: "Look! He wants to be sexually active." I averted my eyes but then opened them again to become an orca voyeur. I watched as the male began to pester (my word) the female. She first gently rebuffed his attentions. He persisted. She became actively hostile; she had a right—she was sixteen months pregnant. Water began to splash around the tank as the female moved quickly away from the randy male. He continued his unwanted attentions— clearly he desired to have sex and probably was hoping he could have an "orcanism." But the female let loose with a cacophony of whale sounds, the splashing in the pool accelerated, and waves reaching four and five feet flowed over the protective wall as the female moved from the "not tonight, dear'" level of refusal to "come near me and I'll sue you for sexual harassment!"

Not one of the human voyeurs left the area, and it was obvious that every woman was cheering the female, while the men couldn't understand why the female orca was reacting the way she did.

After touring other Vancouver highlights, we flew back to Mooseville. I had not expected to go OUT— an Alaskan term meaning "leaving the state"—but was glad that we had visited Vancouver. Unexpectedly I had to go OUT again this month because I had a message on the answering machine from Mount Holyoke College when we returned from Vancouver. I serve on the board of trustees of that Massachusetts college, and a special meeting had been called requiring the trustees to gather in person. So I flew for fourteen hours to participate in a six-hour meeting at the Hartford, Connecticut, airport. Then, quite jet lagged and bleary-eyed, I returned to the boarding gate the next morning for the fourteen-hour flight back to Mooseville. As Shakespeare wrote: "OUT, OUT damned . . ."

Your tired friend sends you
holiday hugs,

Me

January 1995

Dear Friends,

So many of you have sent me newspaper clippings in
the past several weeks, and every one of them dealt
with one topic: KILLER MOOSE. When I had previously written you about how dangerous moose were
to humans, I know you downplayed the seriousness of
my concern. However, now that the major newspaper
syndications have featured the story of the dangers
of moose, you have seen the light (or at least the
newsprint). To allay your hysteria, let me emphasize
that I have not been nor have I seen anyone be charged
by a moose. And since I, myself, am known to be a
heavy charger (just ask my husband, the payer of the
credit card bills), I feel that I can probably hold my
own. If all this verbosity is laughing in the face of the
gods and I become a victim of a stomping moose,
perhaps my tombstone should read: *Dear Lord, please
give this woman full credit with no interest payments,
for she has been charged to death.*

The Inupiaq [Eskimo to you lower forty-eighters]
term for February is *Irraasugruk*, which means "the

month of severe cold." How cold is severe cold? Let me share the fact that several school boards in Alaska have a policy that elementary students are not allowed to go outdoors for recess if the temperature drops to thirty degrees below zero.

Despite the fact that it is not yet February, it has felt very cold outdoors to me in these last few weeks. It is with trepidation that I realize that "very cold" is at least twenty degrees warmer than "severe cold." Nonetheless, I bundled up when we decided to try what the *New York Times* in its December 26, 1994, issue called "one of the fastest growing winter sports." Want to guess? Snowshoeing. Doesn't it sound like the perfect sport for those of us who enjoy sitting by the fire reading a book, or reclining (in a recliner, of course) while watching reruns of *Masterpiece Theatre*? So maybe snowshoeing would not be a "walk in the park" exactly, but rather a "stroll in the snow." Alan and I decided to give it a try.

Before leaving the house, I dressed myself in silk socks topped with thermal socks, silk long johns, jeans, then my super-high-tech "never get wet" snow pants. Higher up, I wore a sweat-wicking T-shirt, a turtleneck, a heavy wool sweater (which I hoped wouldn't confuse the wick-away-sweat T-shirt), followed by a down parka, thick wool mittens, and a full fur hat with earflaps. I was ready to snowshoe, and like Elvis, I left the building to go into our backyard.

For me, any sport has its difficulties, and snowshoeing was no different. The first problem was that I was so bundled up I could not bend over to attach the snowshoes (they looked similar to high-tech surgical equipment) to my boots. To my mind I was a visual twin of Humpty Dumpty; we would have had the same result when we bent over. I had a fall—okay, several falls, and those were just as I was attempting to strap on the snowshoes.

Finally Alan, dressed in far fewer layers (albeit feeling very chilly) strapped me in, and we began the process of moving. Not as easy as the salesperson at the store had claimed: "If you can walk, you can snowshoe." Ha! When I took a step with my right  leg, my foot stepped on top of the left foot's snowshoe, and vice versa. This led to a mincing, rolling, slow gait. Fortunately we had planned to snowshoe around our neighborhood, where people already knew I was "a bit different." I was glad not to run (walk/waddle) into any neighbor because each of my snowshoes was emblazoned with the name of the company that made them, TUBBS. That could have been my ID as well.

We proceeded slowly toward the nearby woods, and everything Robert Frost had written on that topic seemed true to me. First I didn't realize that I was snowshoeing along the top of a high brick wall that was covered with snow—except for the edge of the wall that wasn't. I caught my Tubbs on the exposed brick and took a tumble. Frost wrote, "Something there is that doesn't love a wall." Then miles of snowshoeing later (at least it seemed miles to me), "I had promises to keep." Paramount among them was: *I'll never do this again.*

The longer I minced/waddled in the snow, the warmer I became. First I unzipped my parka and took off my mittens; then I took off my hat. Our neighborhood became strewn with my outer garments. I began to wonder how I could remove some of the under layers of clothing. Alan was far ahead of me and didn't notice the striptease I was doing in the single-digit temperatures. My breath was turning into billows of ice particles each time I exhaled. I managed to shimmy out of my sweater and began to realize I was a "wanton woman" ("wanton" to go back home). In my exhausted delirium I thought about the term *hoar frost*. Did those words describe a nearly naked woman waddling about while her breathing was producing particles of ice on her wick-away-sweat T-shirt?

To distract myself as I sweated and froze and waddled, I thought about all the animals in the woods who had no difficulty walking quickly in the deep snow. The moose that came to eat my flowers and stomped my car a few months ago were surely nearby. Although I did not see any moose, that did not mean they did not see me in my vulnerable state of heat exhaustion and near nakedness. I could not have moved quickly if I had been faced with a mess of moose—a much of moose? A mousse of moose? What is a group of moose called—other than dangerous?

Then far ahead in the distance I saw my husband tilted very precariously and waving his ski poles in the air. He was in trouble! I tried to increase my mincing speed to reach him. It turns out that the salesman's sales pitch, which assured us that aluminum-, titanium-, and neoprene-framed snowshoes will sink no more than a few inches into the snow, was incorrect. Shrubbery hidden by four to five feet of snow can have air pockets underneath that are covered only by a thin veneer of snow. When a hidden air pocket is stepped upon by a snowshoed leg, that leg goes down, down, down until it hits solid snow. But the other leg remains on the surface snow, several feet higher. Alan said it was uncomfortable to say the least and a definite "crotch crusher." Good thing we were not planning on having any more children.

I hate to be a quitter. We paid big bucks for those Tubbs snowshoes, so I might try again sometime. Perhaps I can increase my mincing pace to something approaching a jog. According to the previously mentioned *New York Times* article, snowshoe jogging is what all the glamorous and trendy folk do in Colorado. Melanie Griffith takes a daily winter snowshoe run up Aspen Mountain and is quoted as saying "Snowshoeing lifted my butt about three inches." I'm sure that you are as appalled as I am at that statement—who wants a butt in the middle of one's back?

My New Year's resolution was to cease ending my letters to you with puns BUTT I'm including one that was sent to me by a friend who is always on the lookout for items related to Alaska. Here 'tis: Nanook, the kayak paddler, was training in Alaskan waters. His feet became so cold that to warm them he built a fire in the bow of the boat. The kayak burned and sank. Nanook now knows that you can't have your kayak and heat it too.

As we approach February, I wish you all a Happy Irraasugruk,

Me

February/Irraasugruk 1995

Dear Friends,

It is time for Fur Rondy, a long-time Mooseville tradition celebrating a week in the winter season when all the trappers came into town with their animal pelts to be auctioned and made into various objects of warmth and beauty. (PETA, I am not saying that this is a good thing.) With money in their parka pockets, the trappers would drink, carouse, and make Merry (and whomever else they could find in the red-light district). Just slightly cleaned up and legitimized, Mooseville hosted Fur Rondy (Rendezvous) 1995. Alan and I watched the opening fireworks and the parade of a zillion floats, admired the ice sculptures, and watched showshoe softball games.

Since I never was able to do more than mince slowly on the snow in my snowshoes, I was amazed to see how agile the softball players were as they ran bases and slid into home plate in snowshoes. During the winter in Mooseville, softball is a colorful game. The baseballs are bright orange, and the bases are sprayed neon green. The bright colors allow the players to locate the bases and see the balls against the white snow.

We cheered the teams and cheered ourselves, thinking we were properly attired wearing our new arctic boots and appropriately bundled up against the cold as we walked on all that white snow. Arctic boots are guaranteed to keep feet from frostbite unless the thermometer plummets to 45 degrees below zero. But to our great surprise, what they don't do is give one any traction on ice.

And there was lots of ice. Mooseville had experienced a few days of unseasonable warm weather, and there had been a lot of snow melting until the weather gods remembered that this was Alaska and the temperature was supposed to stay in the single digits. The old snow (*slud* as we Mooseville residents call the mixture of frozen slush and mud) froze into slick, uneven paths and streets, making me extra cautious, walking about one centimeter per step. I watched everyone else walking with quick strides across the slud, and no one was slipping. What was their secret? Spikes. I should not have been surprised—the cars in the winter are accessorized with metal studs; people are accessorized with spikes.

With no reference at all to the opening paragraph above mentioning the red-light district, nor any intent of discussing kinky sexual activities, I will state that the secret to safe walking in the winter here is to have spikes on your rubbers. An oval rubber thing is strapped on to one's boot, and then the six metal spikes that protrude from the rubber thing grip the slud and prevent the person from skidding.

I have changed my mind and now think that perhaps the melting of the many inches of snow in Mooseville these past several weeks was not due to global warming but rather to the all the hot air coming from the elected officials in our Mooseville Assembly, who recently enacted the following law: "No person may engage in a business for hire, either profit or nonprofit, of providing flagellation as a method of massage, unless authorized under license to provide such services as a health care provider . . ." Does this mean that people all over this city have been indulging in flagellation as a profitmaking endeavor? What medical condition would result in a doctor writing a Rx for flagellation? Has frenzied not-for-profit lashing been going on all around me and I have been oblivious? Perhaps I should punish my obtuseness with a little self-flagellation; as I interpret the new law, self-flagellation is still a legal activity.

A perusal of Alaska history does put the flagellation

issue into some historical perspective. During the gold-rush days, most prospectors made their laborious way via the arduous trails of the Yukon and then climbed the perilous Chilkoot Pass to reach the Alaskan Territory. Accompanying them were many women who were going to service the needs of the prospectors (wasn't that said discreetly?). The women carried suitcases filled with tools of their trade. (No, I didn't mean that, Dr. Freud.) Often the men would help the women as they climbed the eight-thousand-foot mountain passes. The men would lend the women ice picks and mountaineering ropes, and for short periods of time during the trip the women would load their suitcases on the dog sleds. But before being of help, the prospectors demanded the right to examine the contents of the women's suitcases. They then only assisted some of the women. Why was that? Well . . . men don't climb passes with women who pack lashes.

The previous paragraph reminds me of a popular Mooseville bumper sticker that alludes to the high proportion of men in the population. Actually, I have read articles from magazines published in the lower forty-eight that encourage women to come to Alaska for a vacation and/or a temporary job and to find a husband. Perhaps the Mooseville chapter of Feminists

United in a Cold Climate (FUCC) designed the bumper sticker that reads: *Alaska: Where the odds are good but the goods are odd.*

Changing the topic slightly from odd men to odd grocery selections, I wanted to tell you about my favorite grocery store here. New Sagaya is a large Asian market that sells everything from kimchi and durian melons to baby eels and pig snouts. They sell freshly made sushi, green-lipped mussels, pickled lamb uteri, and the perhaps the most exotic item of all—Hebrew National kosher hot dogs! What a store! What a city!

Hugs,

Me

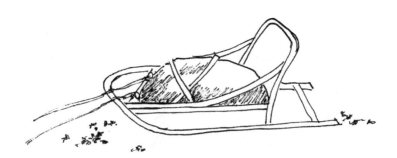

March 1995

Dear Friends,

I have recently returned to Mooseville after spending a few days Outside. Outside is a generic Alaskan term referring to any place other than Alaska. It is very useful, saving the writer from having to spell out the rather tricky names of Massachusetts and Connecticut. I really missed Mooseville and all its excitements, even including the mini earthquakes. Yesterday's trembler was just enough to cause all the many televisions hung on the walls in this rented house to tilt at a rakish angle, the puke-green and mustard-yellow upholstered furniture to skitter away from their normal locations, and the glassware on the shelves to set off a tintinnabulation, not of the bells, bells, bells, but of my yells, yells, yells. I did miss this excitement when I was Outside.

We recently attended the start of the Iditarod dog race that begins in Mooseville and concludes in Nome: a distance of 998 snow-covered miles. The speediest teams can make it in nine or ten days, but not infrequently teams arrive at the finish line fourteen days after they have departed from Mooseville. The packs of dogs were wearing booties on their paws to protect them from ice shards in the hard-packed snow, and I was wearing my arctic boots with thick rubber soles for the same reason. I felt "at one" with the excited dogs. Alan and I were so inspired by the dogs and the enthusiasm of the men competing in the race that we decided that we would someday soon play tourist again and take a dogsled ride of our own. We did, and I learned several surprising things about dog-sledding.

Alan and I reserved an hour's ride. We were each seated in our own sleds, and the musher (the person who drives the sled) stood on the rail of the sled directly behind where we were seated. The first few minutes of the ride were wonderfully relaxing as we traveled over the pristine white snow. But that relaxed feeling ended quickly. The twelve to fourteen huskies that pull each sled are harnessed in pairs, so there are six or seven lines of dogs ahead of the sled. There was much barking, and the dogs kept trying to sniff each other's butts. That undesired activity tended to tangle the lines and jerk the sled around.

Of course, the dogs do not have scheduled bathroom stops; they go on the run. If any of the lead dogs answers the call of nature, there will be other dogs, each with four feet, who are racing past the steaming pile. Each of the dogs' paws takes a little of the rapidly freezing turd along with a bit of icy snow and pushes it backward until the dogs closest to the sled kick it back—directly onto the sled. We didn't expect to have to dodge frozen flying feces, but dodge we did.

The only "feces free" time occurred when we stood with the mushers on the back rungs of the sled. The mushers attempted to teach us the basics of how to mush. The words we were told to remember were *gee, haw, okay,* and *stop.* Unfortunately, I remembered only two words as I led my team directly into the path of some startled cross-country skiers. What came out of my mouth was "Okay! Stop!" Giving contradictory messages to a team of dogs running full-speed ahead is not a good idea. Some of the dogs heard one word, others heard the other word, and each dog acted accordingly while barking, howling, and yelping loudly. Then I said some other words that I hoped were not in the dogs' vocabulary, though my musher was familiar with them.

He then had to calm the dogs down, and led me back to an area where I was told to disem*bark* the sled. I had failed Dog Sled Driving 101. That is a shame, because I remembered so very fondly a radio program of my youth: "Sargent Preston of the Yukon and his Mighty

Husky King." What I don't remember is Sargent Preston ever saying "gee" or "okay." I think he said "Mush, you huskies!" And now for some reason that reminds me of things that transpired during the election of 1972 when Ed Muskie wept in New Hampshire during his presidential primary campaign. Republicans laughed and said, "Hush, Muskie." Did that actually happen, or has time and possible brain damage from flying frozen feces damaged my memory?

Continuing on in this rather convoluted stream of consciousness, I share the thought that the mention of Ed Muskie created a word association with musk ox, and reminds me that I wanted to write you about my wonderful visit to the musk-ox farm near Mooseville. I am a donor to the nonprofit cooperative farm, and thus am an official Friend of the Musk Ox. That status allows me to visit the farm when it would normally be closed to tourists. When I brought some friends who were visiting from the lower forty-eight to the farm, we were taken into the paddocks so we could get nose to nose (should that be our choice) with the female musk oxen. The males were in a separate field, because being deceived by the increasing amount of sunlight, they thought that it was rutting season (that season occurs during the thirteen hours of daylight in the fall, not in the spring.) Since the days were so long, the males, following the honored maxim of *carpe diem*, wanted to seize any female in sight. All the females on the farm—including my friends and me—stayed on the far side of the pasture, a great distance away from the horned and horny male musk oxen.

Another perk of being an official Friend of the Musk Ox is that one can adopt and groom a young musk ox. My adoptee was adorable; her name was Betty.

We bonded over my allowing her to pull and suck the laces on my boots. We had a routine going. I would bend down to retie my laces, and Betty would gently head butt me (a sign of affection, I was told.) Then I would stand up and Betty would grab my laces, suck them for a while, and then try to rip them off my boots. And the process would repeat. After several weeks of visitation, it was time for me to groom Betty, since the weather was getting warmer and her underfur (called *qiviut*) needed to be brushed out. The qiviut is a very soft and dense fur, and is given to some Native tribes for the women to use in knitting gloves, hats, and scarves for sale at the Musk Ox Farm. The big day arrived, and Betty greeted me affectionately. The manager of the farm operations gave me a brush studded with what looked like sharp nails and led us both to a very small wooden pen—so small that Betty couldn't bend down to grab my boot laces without hitting the wall. She was not happy. I could barely turn my body from side to side in there. I was not happy. Since this was such a change from our normal routine, Betty was showing signs of distress . . . and so was I. But there was no one around to help us.

I knew that my job was to remove all the underfur with the brush. I took a deep breath and sang one of our favorite songs: "Baa Baa Black Sheep." I sang, I hummed, I talked about all sorts of things to Betty to distract her from the fact that I was reaching under her belly with something that looked like a medieval implement of torture. As she shimmied and tried to buck, I learned that a brush studded with sharp steel nails could remove a lot of things—fur certainly, but also denim and hand skin. After what seemed like hours, we both were released from the small cubicle. I bent my knee and raised one of my legs to offer my bootlaces to Betty so we could play our game. She looked at me, turned around, and walked away. Alas, the time of innocence was gone.

During the next few months I knew that Betty would be rapidly gaining weight. She would gain close to one thousand pounds eating roots, grass, and flowers in the pastures. A thousand pounds just by eating vegetation—no Ben and Jerry's, no paté, no cheesecake. She would basically only be eating salad without any dressing. Of course with all her dense qiviut fleece, why would she want to dress anyway? Ox me no questions and I'll tell you no lies.

The snow has been melting, and the moose have returned to forage in the yard. Translate that sentence to mean they're stripping the bark off the tree trunks. The correct term for that process is *girdling* the tree, but since the snow is thigh high on the moose, perhaps one should call it "gartering."

Yes, the snow is melting, and that activity is referred to as "breakup" here in Mooseville. Although the lyrics to that old song—"Breaking up is hard to do. Now you know, know that it's true"—refer to romance, they are also valid descriptors of the Great Alaska Breakup. The 121.4 inches of snow we had in our yard have started to melt rapidly. Mooseville now has over thirteen hours of daylight a day, and on some days the high temperatures have reached the forties. Streams of water are rushing down gutter pipes and mini lakes several feet deep have formed in the streets at the bottom of each hill. The grit and mud have thawed and mixed with the melted snow. Because of all the splashing from the roads and driving through the mini lakes, every car on the roads appears to be the same gray/black color. Neither license plates nor windows are visible; however, every car and truck has a small smeared patch of glass where the windshield wipers make a valiant effort to maintain visibility. It is very difficult to identify one's own car in a parking lot, since all the cars look identical in their spring camouflage.

My favorite part of breakup is the archeological aspect of the phenomenon. As the snow melts, objects reveal themselves in a sort of sedimentary layer formation. There is the errant orange plastic–wrapped newspaper thrown by the optimistically named "newspaper delivery person." Then the pitiful, and perfectly preserved by the cold, little birds that never flew south in the fall, but instead flew into windows and, thus stunned, plummeted to the ground, froze, and were covered up by the deep snow. A missing snow shovel has appeared, as has a single woolen mitten. Pieces of wooden fencing knocked down by the snowplow are beginning to periscope their way through the snow at the edge of our driveway. With several more feet of snow left to melt, I am certain that I shall make some important finds. And who knows what large missing objects might be found when Cook Inlet and the Sound, the large bodies of water that surround Mooseville, finally begin to thaw. This raises a question in my mind—so I pass it on to you. What is a frozen sound—"Be Flat" or "Sea Sharp"?

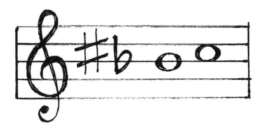

Hugs,

Me

Dear Friends,

This is the month that we change to Daylight Saving Time. As we reset all the clocks, timers, alarms, etc., we wonder why we are doing this. At this season in Mooseville, nobody needs to save daylight. Already it is light from 5:00 a.m. to 9:00 p.m., and the days will grow longer and longer until the summer solstice. Now if there was only a way to actually save the sunlight for when we really need it during the dark days of November, December, January, and February . . . Moonshine can be put in barrels and enjoyed (much to the annoyance of the Feds), so why hasn't someone devised a way to save sunshine?

A friend came from the Deep South to spend a few days with us in the Shallow North. I tried to make sure that she experienced all the highlights of Mooseville. One of those highlights was a visit to the Alaska Native Medical Center. Operated by the Bureau of Indian Affairs, ANMC is a very large hospital complex in Mooseville serving members of the various Alaskan tribes who need medical attention. The complex has a truly wonderful shop where native crafts are sold; there is also a large cafeteria on the campus.

So we went to the Tundra Café for a lunch of native foods. We dined on Athabaskan fry bread and salmon strips that had been hung outdoors on wooden poles to dry. The bread was heavy and greasy, and the salmon had collected miscellaneous bits of flora and fauna on its surface while it was hanging.

My friend selected "Eskimo ice cream" for dessert, even though I, having eaten similar meals during my months in Alaska, had attempted to caution her against the allegedly frozen confection. She refused to believe me when I told her that the ingredient list consisted solely of Crisco, water, and canned blueberries. My skeptical friend asked the cashier about the recipe, and the cashier referred her to the Native American chef behind the cafeteria counter. That man looked her in the eye, smiled, and said, "I use the classic ice cream recipe and add a little sweetened berry juice." My friend glared at me, obviously doubting the veracity of my description. She plopped the dish of dessert onto her tray. We paid and sat at a table to eat lunch. As the only non-Natives in the restaurant, we were the objects of many stares. I whispered to my friend that we needed to appear to enjoy our food selections. "Of course," she said. She decided to eat the dessert first so the ice cream wouldn't melt. I said nothing. I wish you all could have seen her face as she put a large spoonful of Crisco and canned berries into her mouth.

"Swallow and smile," I hissed.

Both actions took enormous effort on her part, but to her credit she declaimed loudly, "Yum." And then even more loudly announced that we had loaded our trays with too much food for lunch and she would focus on eating the protein before any more of her delicious dessert. Proud to call her my friend . . .

Should any of you want to order the dessert, the Native name is akutaq. The word has three syllables, and the middle one is pronounced something like a burp. Are you at all surprised?

It might have been a small, weird karmic connection that caused blue skies and mild weather to occur when my friend Gail visited Mooseville, but then when

Mary Ann was here we had gales. As Mary Ann and I drove down to Seward on the Kenai Peninsula, my car was buffeted (notice the tie-in to the cafeteria story in the previous paragraph) by high winds along the Turnagain Arm (and armpit). Once up into the pass, we encountered a snowstorm.

A few days before my friend had arrived, I'd had the studded tires removed and replaced with the "summer tires." This was entirely the wrong decision—we slipped and skidded as the falling wet snow coated the roads. Several hours later, we arrived at the coastal town of Seward in a full-fledged April gale. All the boats had been secured to the docks, and we were not able to take our scheduled cruise of the Kenai Fjords. We saw a solitary sea lion that was attempting to make its way to the shelter of a nearby cave; then we caved in and had lunch at a local restaurant, and instead of Indian Fry Bread and dried salmon we dined on grilled cheese sandwiches.

When I first began driving my Mooseville car, my husband told me that it had four-wheel drive. I paid no attention to his explanation—after all, all cars have four wheels—and there were too many other new things to which I needed to pay attention during those first few weeks. But braving the elements as we drove the return trip through many inches of snow, skidding and sliding on the deep snow- and slud-covered slippery roads, I pushed a lot of different buttons with images of wheels on them and somehow gained extra traction and was able to reach the safety of Mooseville. Four-wheel drive is a wonderful thing, and I am very glad that my car didn't have only three wheels.

Not surprisingly, after the weather had changed back to blustery snow, my friend who had packed for spring and found herself in winter was cold, and wanted to purchase a warm hat. So we went to a local fur shop to see the latest in Mooseville hat fashion. We wound up spending quite a lot of time in the shop with a lot of deadheads. No, I am not referring to fans of the Grateful Dead: I mean real deadheads. Hats were made of fox, lynx, wolf, beaver, and some that appeared disturbingly like lhasa apso and shih tzu. We're not talking pelts here; the entire animal (innards removed, of course) was made into a hat. Trying one on involved placing the animal's body atop one's own head, the four paws dangling around one's face and the animal's tail hanging down in the back. And jutting forward, in front of one's own face, was the face of the animal. It was infinitely more upsetting to see than a Davy Crockett–type fur cap.

We left that store, and in another, Mary Ann purchased a wool beanie that she wore the remainder of the time she was in Mooseville.

That's all I shall write fur now,

Me

May 1995

Dear Friends,

I now understand why this month is called May. It is due to the fact that people up here in Mooseville start almost every sentence with the utterance "may." As in, "Maybe the trees will leaf out." "Maybe the mud will turn into a green lawn." "Maybe I should put out the porch furniture." Maybe the month should be called Maybe.

At this time of year all the rivers and lakes are rather chilly, but this is prime fishing time. So Alan and I decided to go fishing for a very special type of fish. *Maybe* I'll catch my limit of king salmon. It took Wallis Simpson many years to get Edward VII to renounce his throne for her. It is not easy nor is it a simple matter to catch a king.

We shivered for seven hours in a small, open boat on the raging Kenai River in the attempt to catch one. These magnificent fish weigh over fifty pounds, and at this time of year are just beginning their journey up the rivers. Unfortunately for those attempting to catch them, the salmon choose to arrive when the fishing temperature is forty degrees (because of the icy melted snow waters rushing in the rivers)—not counting the wind-chill factor—and the rivers are moving quickly.

We thought we were prepared with our fishing clothing selections. I wore long underwear and jeans topped with a cotton turtleneck, thick flannel shirt, heavy wool sweater, parka, rubber rain pants, slicker and hat, heavy fishing mittens, and fishing boots. Alan was similarly attired. We were cold. It was difficult to climb in and out of the boat, and the "potty stop" in the woods will not be described here. We caught nothing. I shudder when I remember the discomfort, the long car ride, the expense, the long hours of freezing boredom, and the moments of fear when I thought the boat would capsize in the waves. Yet it will be only forty-eight hours until I return for another attempt to catch a king.

Just call me the Duchess of Windsor.

Earlier this month we had another visitor—a

long-lost relative who has lived in Alaska for over a decade. She fled her hometown of Hoboken, New Jersey (understandable), and went to live in an extremely isolated area of Alaska (not understandable.) Now she and her family live in a small town in the Aleutians by the name of Cold Bay. Can you believe that people would willingly choose to live in a place where the winds blow constantly, the rain is a daily fact of life, and *Alaskans* have named it Cold Bay? Just thinking about it makes me want to put on a sweater.

During the time she has been in Alaska, she has taught in rural villages, married, and lived for ten years in a small cabin that she and her husband built eighty miles northwest of Eagle (the area is described in John McPhee's book *Coming into the Country*), and raised two sons. When the need to socialize and educate the boys became more than the parents could do alone, the family moved out of the bush, as the middle of nowhere is called.

I met my cousin several weeks ago when she took a two-hour plane ride to Mooseville to attend an educational conference. She teaches grades five through twelve in Cold Bay. As a thank-you present for the dinner we had, she sent me her eleven-year-old son for four days. I would have preferred a simple thank-you note.

The boy arrived with a backpack and a bush-person's sense of superiority. (No, that was not a remark derogatory to the political family dynasty in Texas.) Sam carried a sharpening stone in a hand-beaded mooseskin pouch that was attached to his belt. In a leather holder, also attached to his belt, he had a substantial knife.

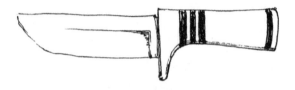

He was never without his belt and accessories because, he said, "One never knows what the future will bring." So true, so true. It was at least a fortnight before I could remove all the Band-Aids on my fingers: as a surprise courtesy, Sam had sharpened—really sharpened—all the kitchen knives.

He is the only eleven-year-old boy I know who does not eat sweets, nor was he keen on fruits or vegetables. He preferred powdered milk to bottled milk and did not like soda. What he loved was pizza and meat—all kinds of meat. We became carnivores for the duration of his visit. After inhaling more than a pound of steak, Sam informed me that although beef was okay, moose was better, beaver was really the best of the red meats, and his absolute favorite meat was beaver liver. He then went on to say, in his most serious voice, that the very best beaver is a young one: sweet, tender, and illegal. (That previous sentence belongs in *Penthouse*, not in *Gourmet*.) When I asked Sam how he knew young beaver was so tasty if it was illegal to kill and eat beaver, I was told that for Native people, it was a legal delicacy. And he had Native status, since he had been born and grew up in the bush. One afternoon we took a walk through the woods adjacent to our house, and I felt totally calm. I had not one worry about whether I would come across a moose or a bear or a beaver. I had Sam and his knife beside me.

It was too bad that our young cousin had already returned to Cold Bay when this year's first grizzly-bear mauling within the Mooseville city limits occurred. Sam would have known how to dispatch the bear with a few backwoods tricks. As it was, the "townie" who was attacked did everything correctly (so said the head of the forest rangers). The "maulee" spoke softly when surprised by the bear, did not make eye contact, lay down on the path, and played dead. The bear, appreciating the Emily Post correctness of the human greeting, reciprocated with a few swipes of his huge clawed paw on the person and gave a gentle bite or two before ambling back off into the woods. The victim is recovering nicely.

Next month Alan and I are spending a weekend in Katmai National Forest. It has the largest population of free-roaming grizzlies in the world. *I must remember the correct greeting behaviors. I must remember the correct greeting behaviors. I must remember the correct greeting behaviors . . .*

I send you (bear) hugs,

Me

June 1995

Dear Friends,

Very few couples can say that on their thirty-first anniversary the earth moved, not only for them but for over 260,000 people. And not just once but several times in one night. Masters and Johnson would rank that as truly amazing. Alan and I will not forget our anniversary evening on May 24 this year in Mooseville. We cowered under my desk in the bedroom, holding on for dear life as the house and ground quivered and quaked at 3:00 a.m. Indeed, it was as if we were atop a giant bowl of Jell-O and someone was shaking the bowl. Each time we returned to our bed to attempt to sleep, another aftershock hit and we would dive back down under the desk. After a while, I began to feel as if I were a tomato in the jellied aspic of life. The following day, the Mooseville News stated that the estimates of the quake's magnitude ranged from 5.5 to 5.7, that the epicenter was a mere twenty-five miles south of Mooseville, and that some of the aftershocks had originated just fifteen miles away. Too close for comfort!

Franklin Delano Roosevelt said, "The only thing we

have to fear is fear itself." Why did I try to follow that advice? My fear of earthquakes has not been reduced by my success in staying safe by cowering under a desk during a substantial earthquake, so what made me think that it would be a character-building event if Alan and I spent a weekend in the grizzly-bear capital of the world? Katmai National Park has an estimated ten to twelve thousand grizzlies within its boundaries. *Ursus arctos horriblilis*—their name says it all. We were advised not to use deodorant, toothpaste, aftershave, perfume; we could use no scents at all. (Of course, if we had any sense, we wouldn't be at Katmai in the first place.)

Another item forbidden for use in the Park is mosquito repellent, despite the fact that the park is a prime mosquito habitat due to all the lakes, streams, and forests. I purchased hats that had mosquito netting along the brim; the netting tied under our chins.

Not surprisingly, the dense netting obscured our vision, which led us to be constantly tripping over the many roots of *Echinopanax horridum,* a sprawling plant with sharp spiked leaves and stems. Each time I tripped and fell, I was able to get a close up view of the bear scat, moose nuggets, and fox feces so abundant in the area.

Once when I was picking myself up, I startled a large blue grouse—a turkey-size bird that waddled off, with me waddling behind with my camera in pursuit of a good photo. Then I remembered that I was in grizzly country and shouldn't wander off. Squinting to see through the netting, I returned to Alan, whose vision was so impaired by the mesh that he never realized that I hadn't been standing near him all the time.

The only way to reach Katmai National Park from Mooseville is by a small plane; the ride takes about two hours. The plane is so small that the airline makes each passenger stand on a large scale with an enormous dial. If that isn't embarrassing enough, the pilot places each person in a specific seat according to one's weight. Whatever my husband wanted to say to me about the poundage I've gained while living in Mooseville I could not hear since we had to wear earplugs for the duration of the flight. Why? So we couldn't hear each other praying and/or whimpering in fear of a crash landing caused by our not being seated in fat person/thin person correct order. Once the little plane landed in the town of King Salmon, a few of us were transferred to a floatplane that seated six people. No one inquired about my weight; maybe the fatter one is, the easier it is to keep the plane afloat. (You know how hefty some Russians are—maybe that is why their airline is named Aeroflot.) Another of my theories is that if one is agile enough to balance walking on the narrow pontoon and then climbing the steep ladder that allows entrance into the cabin of the tiny plane docked in a deep lake, then no matter how much one weighs, one is qualified to be a passenger. Or, for that matter, copilot of the plane . . .

After the six passengers had boarded, the pilot turned to the group and asked, "Which of you wants to copilot?" I've never seen my husband raise his hand so quickly. The fact that Alan's piloting skills were limited to his supervised piloting of a three-seater when we flew to Denali with a friend didn't faze my Lindbergh of a husband. That pilot friend who had Alan take total control of his plane as we flew toward Denali must have had nerves of steel. Or been nuts. He flew a tiny plane he called a Mooney.

I misheard him and thought he said the name of the plane was Looney. Indeed, I thought he was a lunatic to give Alan the controls. I had been strapped tightly into the backseat. With a huge crash helmet on my head, I was unable to communicate with the two men in the front seats. Neither my husband nor the once-and-future pilot could hear what I was saying to them. (And that was a good thing.)

Back to the floatplane adventure . . . The plane "drove off" on the lake's surface and then, like a boat on amphetamines, it increased speed and became airborne. Then it landed on a nearby lake and became a boat again to cruise into the shore. Amazing. Now having left the grizzly-bear area of Katmai for the day, we went to the Land of Ten Thousand Smokes—a park that seemed in name only to be a dream advertising opportunity for the tobacco industry. The volcanic valley is composed of pumice ash and rock hundreds and hundreds of feet deep. No vegetation of any kind can live in such an inhospitable environment. To reach the waterfalls and the deep gorge, we hiked down into the depths of the pumice deposit. The wind whipped the gritty ash that covered the rocks into an ominous tornado-like haze as Alan and I descended down, down, down to the banks of the Lethe (named after the river of forgetfulness in Hades.) I now can blame my poor memory on reaching the Lethe and spending some time on its banks.

After relaxing by the banks of the river, we had to then hike back up the mile or so of steep pumice and rock to regain the road and our transport back to our cabin. Both going down and climbing up we loudly sang the entire time to alert the grizzlies to our presence. Old nursery rhymes, Cole Porter tunes, and Mozart "hums" were the music of our hikes. As we sang, we inhaled mouthfuls of pumice that left us with sore throats and very white teeth. We were desperate to take a shower since we were covered in pumice dust. And because we hadn't been permitted to use deodorant, we smelled a bit whiffy. Perhaps a similar expedition was the creative source for the ad campaign: "Pumice her anything, but give her Arpège"?

During the course of our weekend at Katmai, we were attacked and bitten many times, but only by mosquitos; we saw NO bears at all. FDR was correct. And as Shakespeare wrote, "All's well that ends well."

Barrow is the most northern city in the USA. My husband had been there several times, as well as to the nearby town of Deadhorse. While I had no desire to see Deadhorse (or even think about why the town had been given that name), I was curious to explore Barrow. So in mid June, I flew three hours north toward the Chukchi Sea and the town of Barrow. It is an arid, windy seaside community populated by three thousand Inupiats (one of the five Eskimo tribes). The Inupiats are subsistence hunters and survive on whale, seal, caribou, and the occasional Tex-Mex meal. *Pepe's North of the Border* is the most popular eatery 330 miles north of the Arctic Circle. However, I think that there is a marvelous opportunity for someone to open a second restaurant in the town and name it *Chukchi Cheese Pizza* . . .

Both the Chukchi and the Beaufort Seas that combine to form the Arctic Ocean were still mostly frozen when I visited. Bits of bowhead whales littered the beaches. Both "bits" and "beaches" are misleading terminology. To clarify: a "bit" of a whale is the size of a small VW, and a "beach" here is an area covered with black grit and strewn with rocks bordered by sea water that is frozen in high wavelike mounds.

This year has been a good whaling season, and in celebration of that fact, the natives were able to enjoy lots of mikigaq (a delicacy of fermented whale meat), whale tongue, and muktuk. Because the very name of the delicacy caused a retching sound to come out of my throat, I decided to refrain from eating the mikigaq, but I did munch on the muktuk (Inupiat for whale blubber), which tasted like a combination of escargot, Portobello mushroom, and abalone, with the stringiness of celery occurring from the skin. The taste lingered in my mouth for a long time since the whale skin strands stayed between my teeth. Unfortunately, dental floss was not an item stocked in the only grocery store I could find in Barrow.

Mikigaq, whale meat, other meats, fish, and frozen foods are stored all year long in backyard "freezers"— deep holes cut into homeowners' backyards. The freezer takes the shape of a cylinder in an area excavated ten to twelve feet down into the permafrost. Food is placed on the floor of the "freezer" which maintains a year-round temperature in the low teens. I was fortunate to strike up a conversation with a woman who lived in Barrow, and she offered to show me her freezer. She lifted the heavy wooden disc that covered the opening to the freezer, and I saw a ladder; at the bottom of the ladder were steaks of whale and moose, packages of frozen vegetables, fish, and whale blubber—and to my great delight, boxes of Eskimo Bars!

Barrow has very few trees or shrubs, and little green vegetation of any kind. The area is in total darkness for four months each winter. Garbage litters the dirt streets after the snow has melted, and the wind coming in from the Arctic Ocean whips clouds of dust and bits of garbage around the town. I would think that it could be a very depressing place. It must be depressing even for the lemmings that live in the area and that have worn deep ruts into the tundra. Every several years, thousands of the rodents run in single file and leap off the beach cliffs into the sea.

I didn't see any of the depressed lemmings, nor did I see polar bears. I was told that the polar bears were ten to fifteen miles out on the ice floes, searching for seals and/or eating discarded portions of the whale carcasses left by the Inupiat hunters. But I did see eider ducks and Arctic terns. Did you remember that those birds always travel in pairs because one good tern deserves another?

The Distant Early Warning station is located in

Barrow. The DEW line, a remnant from the Cold War (how aptly named up here), is still occupied by some of our military. Has anyone in the Pentagon remembered that they have stationed people up here? Possibly the guys in the Barrow station should dedicate a folk song to their superiors at the Pentagon: "Oh DEW line, Oh DEW line, oh DEW remember me . . ."

Perhaps there really is a need for the DEW line station to be staffed, even though I had thought that the Cold War was old history. This very month the alarm went out on the radios and televisions all over Mooseville: "It is June eleventh, and it will be legal to kill reds after midnight on the Russian River." A frenzy hit the town, reminiscent of the anticommunist scares of the mid 1950s. Alan and I joined in the fray with our fishing rods in tow and drove down to the banks of the Russian River to try to catch some fish during the first run of the red salmon. Just as J. Edgar Hoover said, "Those bastards are devious and tricky." No success yet.

It is not only red-salmon season; it is tourist season. People have been grumbling as more and more leisure suit–clad tourists with cameras dangling from their necks disembark all over town from huge tour buses that block traffic. It is only June, and I am told that this deluge of "outsiders" will continue for the next several months. Shops will be filled, streets clogged, and trails strewn with Kleenex and candy wrappers. The Mooseville newspaper made this official the other day when on their front page, using the same headline font they use to announce deer- or bear-hunting season, wrote "Tourist Season Has Begun." I have noticed many bumper stickers this month on the cars in Mooseville that put in abbreviated form a sentiment I've heard from residents at dinner parties: *If It's Tourist Season, Why Can't We Shoot Them?* Good question.

Enough for now,

Me

Dear Friends,

There is so much daylight in June that Alan and I are constantly energized and ready to have lots of adventures. So this month I am sending you a second letter describing some of the recent happenings going on in Mooseville and its environs.

Although Alan and I hadn't caught any red salmon, we decided to fish for halibut. Out in the boat at 6:00 a.m. and back to the dock at 6:00 p.m., we caught six twenty-to thirty-pound fish. By the end of the day our arms really ached.

Halibut are large flat fish that are bottom feeders, and they stay at the bottom of the water. Where we were fishing, the bottom of the water was about 250 feet below the boat. Unlike the way to fish taught by Pudge where one casts and the fly stays atop the water, to fish for halibut one puts a sizeable piece of herring on a large hook, attaches a two-pound lead weight, and drops the line down, down, down. After a few minutes, one rewinds the reel and hopes there is a fish on the hook large enough to justify all the winding and bending and stretching.

Alan's big one "got away"—reely. He had her (the larger ones are female) almost to the boat, and we could see the large dark shape in the water, but his line got twisted with another fisherman's line. Then, to our horror, the fishing guide cut Alan's line by mistake. There is now a halibut swimming in Resurrection Bay with a hook and a two pound lead weight attached to her jaw. Can't you just imagine the conversation in the briny deep? Fish talking to her friend: "I don't understand it. I nibble on a little piece of herring and I gain two pounds; I'll need to go to Weight Watchers if I can't get rid of this weight on my own."

During this beautiful time of sunshine, we have taken short excursions and hikes. One day we drove to Hope, a small settlement fifteen minutes from Mooseville as the crow flies, but a two and a half-hour ride as the Ford drives. One would think that Hope would be located just past Expectation and before Despair, but it is actually on the far side of Turnagain Arm. (I'm not sure where anatomically that would place it.)

We had planned to have a picnic and a hike in an area we hadn't explored previously. There is a childhood song that might explain our rationale. "The bear went over the mountain, the mountain, the mountain to see what she could see. The bear went down the mountain, the mountain, the mountain with a little bear behind."

We drove up an abandoned mine road for miles, up, up, up the mountain, fording several streams. If we hadn't been driving a Ford Explorer, we'd have been Dodging the water . . . We walked a bit, had our picnic, and then wanted to "use the facilities." Of course there were no facilities, so we went into the woods; and for just a few moments we each had a *little bare behind.*

Another day we went to Hatcher Pass for a hike to some gold mines that are still operative. As we walked, we came to areas where the snow was still two feet deep! Despite the snow on the ground, the mosquitoes were swarming everywhere.

Alaska has twenty-seven varieties of mosquitoes, and seventeen species live in the Hatcher Pass area. I

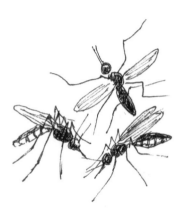

had covered myself with repellent that worked for about five minutes until one species penetrated the spray coating and lived to tell the others about it. I guess their communication would be known as the buzzword . . .

In an earlier letter I had written you that I had felt a kinship with Wallis Simpson in the quest to get a king. I finally caught a king salmon. But it was a small one, so I assume that it was a future king—a prince. I named the fish Charles, and now I identify with Princess Diana. Although the excitement and glory lasted for a few hours, the experience wasn't half as grand as I thought it would be. My fish was 34.7 pounds; "real" kings weigh between fifty and sixty pounds. However, after spending endless hours trying to catch anything at all, I was pleased to have caught a member of piscine royalty.

Our most recent visitors journeyed to Mooseville from Houston so they could fish and sightsee and determine whether all the things I have written in my letters were true. They agreed that I have been understated in my descriptions. Certainly I know they will verify the following story about our time in Talkeetna. Located near Denali, the town of Talkeetna is on the highway that runs between Mooseville and Fairbanks. Since it is almost a midway point between the two cities, there are a number of places to stop, gas up the car, and get coffee. The most memorable of those places is named Skinny Dick's Halfway Inn. We decided to get our lunch at a different café.

The town has only a few hundred residents and is the starting point for many of the climbing expeditions to Denali, officially known as Mount McKinley. The tiny town has a distinctly 1960s feel, with a laid-back flower-child atmosphere. From the conversations we overheard, it would seem that everyone had named their daughters Mary Jane and that the residents appreciate having lush green lawns because they kept referring their friends to shops where one can buy the best grass.

Each year Talkeetna holds a Moose Dropping Festival. No, the large animals are not dropped from great heights to amuse the onlookers; rather moose nuggets (turds, to you non-Alaskans) that have been shellacked and numbered are dropped by airplane onto a field. The nugget closest to the target painted on the field is the winner. Five hundred nuggets are individually painted by the members of the local VFW. I guess the veterans chose to do this as their annual fund raiser instead of the more conventional bake sale. I put money on nugget #64, and our friends are rooting for their own piece of shit, #147.

Alas, we shan't be returning to Talkeetna later on this summer to actually see the Big Drop or take part in other festivities. I greatly regret that we won't be returning, because during a conversation at the lunch counter someone suggested that I would make a good participant in the festival's Big Mountain Momma contest.

The reason that we won't be back in Talkeetna is because we will be returning to Houston in July. We don't know how long we will stay there, or the details of my husband's new job. When I complain that we are being moved around as if we were pawns on a giant chessboard, I am reminded that the "game" is ours to play as we choose, but I should remember that we already have caught the kings.

Sending you "royal" hugs,

Me

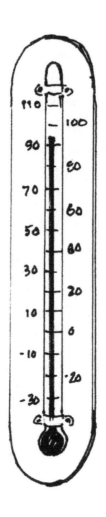

Epilogue

September 1995

My dear Alaska friends,

I can't believe it's been three months since I left Anchorage. Has Termination Dust come to the Chugach Mountains? I have so many more questions for you, things that didn't occur to me to ask when we were together in Mooseville. Perhaps in your letters to me you would explain why so many Alaskan rental cabins and motels position a large bathtub in the center of the bedroom, or why in early December some official-looking truck drove down our street and hosed down all the front yards and the fir trees with Eau de Skunk. No matter how much you all tried to teach me, I still am unsure whether I could correctly identify a black bear from a brown bear so that I would be able to react correctly—e.g. playing dead on the ground with my arms over my head or standing tall while slowly walking backward. Before I return to visit you, I will need to figure that out.

Speaking of bears and "unbearable"—that word would describe the temperature in Houston. Today when I went to buy groceries, the temperature reading in my car was 93 degrees.

The humidity is so high that my hair is in ringlets; I look like an elderly version of Shirley Temple. (And my own temples are agleam with perspiration.) Alan and I have settled back into our house and I have been greeted by "my" palmetto bugs, as well as our neighborhood family of copperhead snakes. I'm missing the Three Mooseketeers. They may have stomped, but at least they didn't slither. Rather than write each of you individually I think I will write a group newsletter letting you know of my adventures here in the Deep South.

So . . . stay tuned, and get your mailbox ready for issues of *Hot Flashes: Scribbles from Swamp City.*

Hugs,

Me

Acknowledgments

So many people unknowingly inspired me to write this book; for years people urged me to put down my camera and start writing. And now I have done so . . . My friends who were role models for this writing endeavor include: Kit Tapers Wallingford, Jane Silverman Grossman, Diane Atkinson, Marty Sherwin, Mary Ann Weil Sternberg, Lois Farfel Stark, Wendy Wasserstein, Charles Burson, Richard Pesikoff, Catherine O'Connell, Mona Marich Hanford, Edward Djerejian, and Peter Ascoli.

Those whose love of puns and word play provided me with a lifetime of laughter include: Richard Bernicker, Victor Ringel, Matthew Ringel, Harrington Van Epps, Patrick Hughes, and Paula Ross Hoffman.

Those who cheered me on and read or patiently listened to endless reading and rereading of chapters include: Gail Carver Faris, Elizabeth Tarlau Weingarten, Phyllis Childress, Linda Green Sandrich, Barbara Greenfield Samuels, Diane Ley Espinoza and my wonderful friends from two groups: the Possets and the Yaks.

Unknowingly, Alice Gardner Boreta and Gretchen Beck Green, both alumnae of Mount Holyoke College, gave me the impetus to create this book based on the letters of Kitty Eppston.

Betsy Thorpe, both a consummate professional and a friend, patiently walked me through each of the many steps needed to reach publication. I greatly value her experience, wisdom, and gently given advice.

Anne Lamkin Kinder's brilliant artistic ability brings a wonderful dimension of humor and delight to this book.

Kudos to Diana Wade for the creation of the cover of this book and for its interior layout—both will bring delight to the reader. In addition, Diana patiently answered all my questions and clarified all the technological stuff that too frequently left me very puzzled. Kudos also to Maya Myers for her extraordinarily keen eye and prompt turn around and responses to my myriad questions.

And to my husband Richard who has been my cheerleader for many decades I give great thanks for his endless patience and support for all parts of this endeavor.